Mastering The Mental Side Of Basketball

Hemispheric
Kinesiology

Ernest Solivan

Mastering The Mental Side of Basketball

ISBN: 978-0-6151-7233-0

"I have missed more than 9000 shots in my career. I have lost almost 300 games. On 26 occasions I have been entrusted to take the game winning shot...and missed. And I have failed over and over and over again in my life. And that is why... I succeed."

Michael Jordan
Chicago Bulls

Mastering The Mental Side of Basketball

Mastering The Mental Side of Basketball

Table of Contents

Table Of Contents

Introduction

With the advent of quantum physics, science must now acknowledge that there are things that happen below our level of conscious awareness that dramatically affect the experiences we create. Mastering The Mental Side Of Basketball is a book designed to work on a quantum level, or below your level of conscious awareness. That is where the blockages are preventing you from reaching your full potential to become a better player.

The first part of the book explains the development of Hemispheric Kinesiology(HK) and provides a foundational context on how your mind and brain influence the experiences (both positive and negative) you create on and off the court. The second part explains how to use HK to become the kind of player you would like to become.

This is a book about HK and how you can use it to achieve peak performance as a basketball player. HK is a muscle testing technology that allows me to access, isolate and change undesirable subconsciously stored information preventing athletes from achieving peak performance.

HK most salient characteristic is that it offers a very credible, rational and viable explanation as to why you experience performance problems during competition and offers a remedy that will allow you minimize and/or eliminate those problems so that you may play to the best of your ability.

There is an old saying that you cannot teach an old dog new tricks. This is a testament to how difficult change is for just about everyone. There are basically three elements necessary to create change in your life. They are Sensation, Perception and Conception. Sensation is the capacity to experience; Perception is the capacity to be aware of what you are experiencing; and Conception is taking action to begin the process of change, or it can also represent a rebirthing into some new experience.

I refer to HK as "A Language Of Change" because it embodies all the elements necessary to facilitate and accelerate positive change in the athletes who experience it. HK does not diagnosis or label. Please respect the context in which I present this extraordinary and very effective discipline. It works on the simple premise that if it stresses you to play basketball, you are not going to do it well.

Please set aside your prejudices, beliefs and judgments and do your best to keep an open mind. HK is a little different twist on psychology. This discipline was created with the intention of allowing you to help yourself facilitate and accelerate positive changes that will immeasurably improve the quality of your life on the basketball court, as well as in your personal life. And, isn't that what we are all looking for?

It is said that basketball is 95% physical and 5% mental. When you have finished reading

Mastering The Mental Side Of Basketball you will understand why basketball is 100% mental.

The Mind

When you set a goal to do something, one of two things will happen. You will either succeed or fail. What determines your success or failure is the information contained in your Mind. This stored information is the information you will use while attempting to accomplish your goal.

If the information in your Mind supports you in successfully completing your goal, the accomplishment of your goal will be easy and almost effortless. However, if the information in your Mind does not support you in successfully accomplishing your goal, the accomplishment of your goal will be very difficult and require a tremendous amount of effort.

The Mind is generally thought to be the seat of consciousness. It is made up of every aspect of our being. There are many philosophies that view the Mind in a way that has created numerous fragments, i.e., the spiritual mind, the emotional mind, the etheric mind, etc. I found all these subdivisions to be very confusing.

In HK I rely upon the very old axiomatic metaphysical concept known as "cause and effect." Several of the theories that support cause and effect are, "for every action there is an equal and opposite reaction;" "water seeks it own level;" and "what goes around, comes around."

When we are dealing with the Mind we are dealing with something we cannot see. Although I cannot see a basketball player's

Mind, I can see the experiences that Mind is creating. For instance, if I am working with a player who can only score 8 points a game, I must assume that he has information stored in his Mind to support him in scoring 8 points a game or he would be doing something else.

It is important to note that your Mind supports you in everything you do. If you can only score 8 points a game, your Mind is supporting you, and it is doing so based upon information it has stored in its memory banks relating to your per game point average. Your physical body is merely acting out (i.e., 8 points per game) based upon this stored information, and it does it automatically.

To understand cause and effect, you must first understand that before anything physically happens in your life, it must first start as a thought. So, if you want to change the undesirable experiences you are creating, you must change the thoughts that are responsible for creating those undesirable experiences.

For example, the information stored in the player's Mind is the "cause" (mental limitation or blockage) while the experience he is creating (8 points per game), is the "effect." The player is creating this experience because his physical body is responding by corresponding to information stored in his Mind. The intention of the HK program is to provide players with a resource that will allow them to create positive change and help them achieve peak performance during competition.

Before I explain how this is accomplished, it is important to establish a context and foundation whereby all the contributing factors to this performance phenomenon may be examined and understood. It is noteworthy to point out that in HK all we are dealing with is information. For example, although an emotion is something we can feel, it is stored in the Mind as information.

The Mind has two parts. The Conscious Mind and the Subconscious Mind.

The Conscious Mind

The Conscious Mind is known as the "knower" because it has the ability to be aware of itself. It has the capacity to be aware of what it is thinking and feeling in the normal waking state. It also has the ability to know what it is doing and why. One of the major functions of the Conscious Mind is its use of volition. Volition is defined as, "the act of using the will; exercise of the will as in deciding what to do; a conscious or deliberate decision of choice thus made."

You are where you are in your life right now as a direct result of the choices you have made using the volitional part of your Conscious Mind. The Conscious Mind provides us with short-term memory and can only focus on one thing at a time. The Conscious Mind uses the five senses; sight, hearing, smell, taste and touch, to collect information which allows it to experience awareness.

The Conscious Mind uses this collected information to formulate your self-image, your prejudices, and your belief system. The most important function of the Conscious Mind is that it exercises it volitional capabilities by allowing us to set goals. The information collected by the Conscious Mind will influence the formulation and successful completion of the goals we set throughout our lives.

So, what happens when the Conscious Mind, using its volition, decides to engage in some particular activity like basketball? Well, it types out a mental memo of instructions and sends it to your Subconscious Mind.

The Subconscious Mind

When you engage in a particular activity, such as basketball, it is the responsibility of your Conscious Mind to decide the nature of the activity. Your Conscious Mind will send instructions to your Subconscious Mind, "Send me all the information you have relating to basketball."

If the information accessed from your Subconscious Mind relating to basketball is supportive, you will perform the activity easily and efficiently. However, if the information accessed from your Subconscious Mind is not supportive or contradicts the goal set by your Conscious Mind, your activity will become very difficult and require a tremendous amount of effort.

The Subconscious Mind is a part of the Mind known as the "doer" because it merely does what it is programmed to do. Unlike the Conscious Mind, the Subconscious Mind does not have the capacity to exercise volition or choice, it simply "does."

The Subconscious Mind acts out through the physical body and uses information it has stored in its memory banks relating to the particular activity (basketball). This "acting out" is done instantaneously and automatically. This stored information arrived into the Subconscious Mind through the Conscious Mind using the five senses (sight, hearing, smell, taste, and touch).

To more fully understand this acting out

phenomenon, remember when you were a child learning how to tie your shoes? At first it required a tremendous amount of time and concentration. Now, you do it without consciously thinking because it has become a subconscious act. The same thing happens when you take the court. Your physical body automatically acts out base upon information obtained from your Subconscious Mind relating to everything from your self-image to your per game point production.

The Subconscious Mind is a storage facility for all information that enters through the Conscious Mind. The one important feature to note about the Subconscious Mind is that when it is storing information it is impersonal. It doesn't say, "I am not going to store this experience because it was a bad experience." IT STORES EVERYTHING!

The Subconscious Mind also provides us with long-term memory, and is where our belief system is housed. If you have information stored that you can only score 8 points a game, your physical body will reciprocate by only allowing you to score 8 points a game. Additionally, the Subconscious Mind does not have a sense of humor and cannot distinguish between something real or imagined.

If you don't believe me, try telling someone who has a fear of heights that they have nothing to be afraid of. You can clearly see how powerful our beliefs are, and that they have a tremendous influence, both positive and negative, over the decisions we make throughout our lives.

The Subconscious Mind can be likened to the hard drive of your computer with one notable exception. When using a computer, you have the option of saving or erasing the information on your screen. Every piece of information that enters the Subconscious Mind is stored for future use.

Your Conscious Mind will eventually use this subconsciously stored information when it engages in an activity that corresponds to the information in storage. The Subconscious Mind will provide the Conscious Mind with whatever information it has available. The information can be supportive or non-supportive in nature.

When subconsciously accessed information is non-supportive, the physical body will manifest stress. For instance, let's say you set a goal to score 20 or more points in an upcoming game, and the information you have stored subconsciously is that you are only capable of scoring 8 points a game. Your physical body will immediately manifest stress.

Your Subconscious Mind is basically telling your Conscious Mind, "I do not have the information stored to support you in scoring 20 or more points a game, however, I do have information stored to support you in scoring 8 points a game." The end result - 8 points per game.

WHENEVER THERE IS CONFLICT BETWEEN THE CONSCIOUS MIND AND THE SUBCONCIOUS MIND, THAT CONFLICT WILL ALWAYS MANIFEST IN THE PHYSICAL BODY AS STRESS!

It's as if the Conscious Mind and the Subconscious Mind are not on the same page. When stress is present in the physical body, it will always weaken the body. It is when your physical body is in this weakened state during a game, that you will miss an easy shot that you have made 100s of times in practice.

It's as if your physical body goes on red alert because the information in the Conscious Mind (20 points per game) does not match the information accessed from the Subconscious Mind (8 points per game). The Subconscious Mind, acting out through the physical body, will do everything in its power to sabotage any point production over 8 during your game.

There is a very integral component of the Mind that gets involved when the Conscious and the Subconscious Mind interact. It is known to as the "Critical Factor."

The Critical Factor

After information enters the Conscious Mind, it is reviewed prior to storage in the Subconscious Mind. The responsibility for this task belongs to a component of the Mind known as the Critical Factor. The Critical Factor literally criticizes or reviews information that comes into conscious awareness. After its review, the Critical Factor must make a decision regarding the disposition of the information. The Critical Factor has two options. It can either store the information, or reject it.

Everyone knows that the color of the sky is blue, but suppose I told you that the color of the sky was red. When that statement enters your Conscious Mind, your Critical Factor will stop it momentarily and says something to the effect, "Let me check the information I have in subconscious storage relating to the color of the sky." The Critical Factor checks and discovers that the information stored in the Subconscious Mind indicates that the color of the sky is blue. The Critical Factor proceeds to reject the statement, "The sky is red."

Let's also suppose that the 8 point per game player sets a goal to score 20 points a game. His Conscious Mind will send instructions to his Subconscious Mind, "Send me all the information you have stored relating to scoring 20 points per game." His Critical Factor will stop this information before it hits the Subconscious Mind and say something to the effect, "Let's see what kind of information we have in subconscious storage relating to 20 points per game."

The Critical Factor checks and discovers that the information stored indicates that the player can only score 8 points per game and proceeds to reject the statement. It's as if the Critical Factor instructs the player's Subconscious Mind to go on "red alert" and proceeds to sabotage any attempt this player may make to score more than 8 points per game.

The subconsciously stored information (8 points per game) will remain until the player changes the information. That is exactly what HK will help you do.

Imagine the Critical Factor as a guard, and that it is guarding all information coming into and leaving the Mind. How do you change this information? How do you change subconsciously stored information preventing you from achieving peak performance on the court? In order to change subconsciously stored information, we must achieve Critical Factor Bypass.

Critical Factor Bypass

Critical Factor Bypass occurs when new information is allowed to bypass the Critical Factor of the Mind in an effort to change old information stored in the Subconscious Mind. HK can achieve Critical Factor Bypass, which enables you to literally change subconsciously stored information. Using HK to achieve Critical Factor Bypass allows us to accelerate change for the athletes who experience it. In order to more fully understand Critical Factor Bypass, we must first look to the advertising industry.

On many occasions advertising agencies will send sales copy to a psychologist, and ask, "Will this copy achieve Critical Factor Bypass for our product?" The ad agencies know that if they can achieve Critical Factor Bypass on anyone who hears or sees their commercials, their chances of selling their product or services are greatly enhanced. They carefully choose the people who star in these commercials, carefully choose the wording, and carefully choose the scenarios.

How can they motivate someone to buy their product or service? One way to do it is using fear in the form of authority figures. It cannot be done blatantly. It must be subtle. Have you ever noticed that in many commercials ad agencies will use policemen, judges, doctors, or firemen. All these professions represent authority figures and the ad agencies know that when a policeman tells you to do something, you normally do it without question. You do what you are told because the policeman was able to achieve Critical Factor Bypass.

Another very subtle tactic ad agencies will use to create Critical Factor Bypass is race and gender. I once saw a print ad that contained a Caucasian, an African-American, an Asian, an older gentleman, an older woman, a young man, and a young woman. They covered a lot of bases with that ad. And, it was all done subjectively or subconsciously.

Sometimes the ad agencies will appeal to your emotions. I am certain you have seen the Michelin Tire commercial with a baby sitting in a tire. That commercial has been running for years. This particular commercial has been successful because the ad agency was able to achieve Critical Factor Bypass by using the baby to appeal to the emotions of the viewer. Michelin must be selling a lot of tires or they would not continue to use this very effective commercial.

Some of the other tactics used by ad agencies are humor, sex and money. In fact, the next time you view or hear a commercial advertisement, ask yourself, "What are they doing in this commercial to achieve Critical Factor Bypass?" I will explain in a later chapter how we are able to achieve Critical Factor Bypass using HK so that the 8 point per game player can become a 20 point per game player.

For now, we have examined the nuances of the Mind to include the Conscious Mind, the Subconscious Mind, the Critical Factor, and Critical Factor Bypass. The Mind must act out through the physical body and it does this using the Brain.

The Brain

Although the Mind is the decision maker, it is the brain's responsibility to carry out those instructions. The brain is a part of the Central Nervous System composed of approximately 10 billion nerve cells. Each cell is linked to one another, and together they are responsible for the control of all functions in the physical body. The brain disseminates these instructions throughout the physical body using information provided by the Mind in the form of electrical impulses.

The brain is an organ consisting of three major components. The Left Hemisphere, The Right Hemisphere and the Corpus Callosum. Although these three components are integral, they each have very specific and different functions, and two of these components can function independently should the need arise. The Left Hemisphere of the brain controls the right side of the physical body, while the Right Hemisphere controls the left side.

We need only look at a stroke victim to understand this phenomenon. Notice that in the majority of the cases only one side of the body is paralyzed. That's because the hemisphere of the brain on the opposite side of the affected area was so severely damaged during the stroke that it manifested as paralysis.

The corresponding side of the subject's physical body is not receiving electrical impulses (information) from the damaged hemisphere resulting in partial or total paralysis. There are degrees of dysfunction between the brain and the physical body, and that total paralysis represents the extreme.

Since the Left and Right Hemispheres of the brain can function independently and have their own responsibilities, they need some way to communicate. This is accomplished using the Corpus Callosum. The Corpus Callosum is a band of nerve fibers that connect the Left and Right Hemispheres of the brain. The hemispheres share and exchange information (electrical impulses) that will eventually be disseminated to the physical body.

I realized in my research in working with athletes that the hemispheres of the brain have a tendency to "weaken" or "switch off." When one hemisphere is switched off, the opposite hemisphere will dominate. For instance, if your Left Hemisphere is switched off, your Right Hemisphere will dominate whatever activity you may be involved in, and vice versa. The hemispheres of the brain are continually influenced by and are reacting to stimuli in your immediate external environment.

The brain does basically three things. It processes (learns), stores, and disseminates information. What kind of information? That would be any and all information relating to pictures, sounds, fragrances, culinary data, and touch. All three of the major components of your brain come into play when the brain is exercising these functions. Let's first examine the Left Hemisphere of the brain.

The Left Hemisphere

When the Left Hemisphere of the brain processes (learns) information, it only understands words, language and numbers. That's because the Left Hemisphere processes information sequentially, or one piece at a time. The Left Hemisphere is one-dimensional, and can only focus on one thing at a time. The Left Hemisphere controls the right side of the physical body and it accomplishes this by sending information in the form of electrical impulses.

When the Left Hemisphere of the brain weakens or switches off, during the processing or learning stage, it's as if a short circuit occurs in the electrical field in the physical body, and the incoming information never reaches the hemisphere of the brain that is switched off. Incoming information will only store in the hemisphere that is switched on.

For instance, if your Right Hemisphere is switched off while your brain is learning, the incoming information will store in your Left Hemisphere. Now, because there was no information stored in your Right Hemisphere, when it's time for your brain to disseminate the information to you at some point in the future, you will only receive information from your Left Hemisphere. It's as if you are only getting half the information.

When the Left Hemisphere of the brain stores information, it will only store sequential information such as words, language and numbers. It will store information that is logical and organized. In other words, the information stored in the Left Hemisphere must be structured.

When the brain disseminates information to the physical body, the Left and Right Hemispheres deal with different and specific information. The Left Hemisphere of the brain provides the physical body with the following information, attributes and qualities:

Logic, action, decision making, critical, one-dimensional, mechanical, compulsive, doubt, cautious, judgmental, hard working, limitation, shame, rational, stoic, organization, reasoning, specificity, structure, cold, unfeeling, boundaries, rules, rigidity, opinionated, intense, impersonal, introverted, controlled, predictable, restricted, precise, serious, conservative, quiet, hard, intolerant, auditory, scientific, temporal (the now), arrogant, skeptical, fearful and finite.

When you engage in an activity and the Right Hemisphere of your brain is weak or switched off, your physical body is only receiving information, or a majority of the information, from your Left Hemisphere. This causes you to become left-brain dominant while you are engaged in that particular activity. This results in your exhibiting one or more of the personality traits listed above.

For example, a left-brain dominant individual is introverted, dresses conservatively, and is very structured. The problem is that the left brain dominate individual does it to excess.

I believe this switching off anomaly is one reason that science speculates that we only use 10% of our brain. Now let's examine the Right Hemisphere of the brain.

The Right Hemisphere

When the Right Hemisphere of the brain processes information, it only understands movement and pictures. That's because the Right Hemisphere is spatial and can process information collectively rather than sequentially. This collectiveness allows it to process large amounts of information at one time.

For instance, if you were looking at a picture of a landscape with your Left Hemisphere, you would have to look at every piece of the picture individually because the Left Hemisphere processes information sequentially. You cannot see the whole picture if you are only looking at one piece. The collective capabilities of the Right Hemisphere allows you to see the whole picture, while the Left Hemisphere provides you with the capacity to structure the collective information in the form of discernible images.

When we examine this phenomenon during the learning stage of our development, we can clearly see how the hemispheres of the brain influence how we learn. Let's look at an elementary school student named Harold. He is learning to read the sentence, "See Jack jump." If Harold had the Right Hemisphere of his brain weak or switched off while reading this sentence, his Left Hemisphere would dominate.

Now, Keeping in mind that the Left Hemisphere processes information sequentially, Harold's Left Hemisphere will know and understand the words see, Jack, and jump. However, because his Right Hemisphere is weak or switched off, he will have difficulty achieving total comprehension. In order for that to happen, he would have to send the information from his Left Hemisphere, via the corpus callosum, to the Right Hemisphere, and request additional information such as a visual of a boy jumping. With both hemispheres of his brain participating in the learning process, Harold will achieve total comprehension, no matter what he is learning.

When the brain disseminates information to the physical body, the Right and Left Hemispheres deal with different and specific information. The Right Hemisphere of the brain provides the physical body with the following information, attributes and qualities:

Feelings, emotions, relaxation, beliefs, creativity, flexibility, physical movement, tolerance, visualization, artistic, spatial, self-esteem, forgiveness, no boundaries, unstructured, generalizations, procrastination, compassion, optimism, passivity, funny, unreasonable, loud, expressive, foolish, passion, charming, humility, intuition, love, uncontrollable, multi-dimensional, imagination, addictions, lazy, laid back, open-minded, unorganized and infinite.

When the Left Hemisphere of your brain is weak or switched off, the Right Hemisphere will dominate your activities, from your decision making to your personality. Since your physical body is only receiving information from the

Right Hemisphere of your brain, you will exhibit one or more of the above listed personality traits and attributes. Think of the many times you have procrastinated in your life, or how many times have you been very passionate about a particular cause? It is during those times when the Right Hemisphere of your brain was dominating your thinking. The problem, again, is that you will do it to excess because there is no structure (Left Hemisphere).

The objective in HK is to switch on both hemispheres of your brain in relationship to a thought, statement or action. Having both hemispheres of your brain switched on insures that you will have access to information such as judgment, analysis and structure (Left Hemisphere), as well as creativity, imagination and intuition (Right Hemisphere). With both hemispheres of your brain providing your physical body with information, you will experience total balance in your life no matter what the activity.

A great analogy for explaining hemispheric balance is water. The Right Hemisphere can be likened to boiling hot water, while the Left Hemisphere is ice-cold water. By themselves, their temperatures are very uncomfortable. However, when you mix them together, you get a warm, comfortable and balanced temperature. When both hemispheres of your brain are switched on, you enter a mental space that athletes refer to as "The Zone."

Another salient difference between the hemispheres worthy of note is that the Left Hemisphere deals with "old" information, while the Right Hemisphere deals with "new" information. This influences how the hemispheres of your brain will handle a specific task. Let's assume that you have just purchased something that requires assembly.

The Left Hemisphere of your brain will approach the task by saying something like, "Where are the instructions to this thing (?); I can't put this together without the directions!" Remember that because the Left Hemisphere is using "old" information, it is basically asking, "Show me the way someone else did it, then I can do it."

Conversely, the Right Hemisphere will approach that same task by saying, "Hey, even if we don't have the instructions, let's put it together anyway." That's because the Right Hemisphere is providing the physical body with "new" information in the form of "creativity," and will figure it out eventually. The Right Hemisphere will risk (no instructions), while the Left Hemisphere will tend to play it safe (must have instructions).

Let's take this condition on court. If you are a left brain dominant player (right hemisphere switched off), you will have a tendency to play it safe. You will pass the ball rather than take a shot that you could have made. If you are right brain dominant (left hemisphere switched off), you may take a low percentage shot rather than pass the ball to an open man.

When you can function on court with both hemispheres of your brain strong or switched on, you will achieve a level of play most players just dream of. With access to structure, judgment and organization (Left Hemisphere), and creativity, intuition and imagination (Right Hemisphere), every decision you make supports you in achieving peak performance as an athlete.

In HK it is imperative that we know what activity is taking place in the physical body in relationship to a statement, thought or action. This is accomplished using Muscle Testing.

Muscle Testing

There are three vital pieces of information necessary in HK relating to a statement, thought or action. First, muscle testing allows me to determine whether the physical body is weak or strong relating to the subject matter.

Secondly, muscle testing allows me to determine the condition of the hemispheres of the brain. Thirdly, muscle testing allows me to post test a player to determine the condition of the hemispheres of the brain upon completion of a session.

Muscle testing is a technique that has been widely used in the alternative health field for years and has been used in a variety of applications. I use muscle testing to determine whether stress is present in the player's physical body relating to a statement, thought or action. Since the physical body is merely acting out based upon information contained in your Subconscious Mind, muscle testing allows me to tap into that subconsciously stored information.

In his book "Switching On," Dr. Paul Dennison defines muscle testing as:

"Muscle testing is the art of isolating and testing one muscle at a time in order to determine if it is 'weak' or 'strong', relative to the strength of the individual being tested."

There are forty-two muscle groups in the physical body. In HK, I muscle test the deltoid muscle. The deltoid is the larger triangular muscle of the shoulder, which raises the arm away from the side. If you held your right arm straight out from your side, parallel to the ground, and lifted your arm upward from that point, it is the deltoid muscle that allows you to execute that movement.

When I muscle test someone I will ask them to:

1. Stand with weight evenly distributed on both feet;
2. I have the subject hold his left or right arm straight out or parallel to the ground;
3. I face the subject standing in front of the outstretched arm;
4. I ask the subject to look straight ahead and extend the fingers of his outstretched arm so that they are parallel to the ground;
5. I place my left hand on the subject's left shoulder for support;
6. I place my right hand, using only two fingers (index and middle fingers) on top of the subject's outstretched arm between the elbow and wrist;
7. The subject is now ready to be muscle tested;
8. I will ask the subject to resist upwards slightly, towards the sky, while I apply about 2 ounces of pressure downward towards the ground. This allows both the subject and I to get a feel for the muscle test.

The key to muscle testing effectively is 2-2-2. Use two fingers, apply two ounces of pressure, and hold for two seconds. There are two possible responses to a muscle test. "Strong" or "weak."

A strong muscle test indicates that my downward pressing motion was unable to budge the subject's arm. A strong muscle test also indicates that there was no stress present in the subject's physical body relating to the statement, thought or action for which I muscle tested.

A weak muscle test indicates that the subject was unable to resist my downward pressure, and could not hold his arm parallel to the ground. A weak muscle test is evidence that stress was present in the subject's physical body relating to the statement, thought or action for which we muscle tested.

What does a strong vs a weak muscle test tell me, if anything? Well, if I had had a player make the statement, "I consistently score 20 points per game," the strong muscle test signifies that the player's physical body would totally support him in scoring 20 points per game. The absence of stress in the player's physical body indicates that there is information stored in his Subconscious Mind that would support him in scoring 20 points per game, and he will do it well.

On the other hand, had the player muscle tested weak to the statement relating to 20 points per game, the weak muscle test indicates the presence of stress in the player's physical body relating to the statement. It basically stressed the subject to say, "I consistently score 20 points per game." The weak muscle test tells me that the information stored in the player's Subconscious Mind would not support him in scoring 20 points per game.

A weak muscle test is the physical body's way of saying, "I am not doing that because I do not have information stored in my memory banks to support the activity, or that the information I have stored contradicts whatever it is you want to do (20 points per game)."

The second piece of information I can obtain using muscle testing is the condition of the Right or Left Hemispheres of your brain in relationship to a statement, thought or action. For instance, when checking the condition of the Left Hemisphere, I merely touch the left side of your head and muscle test. If I record a strong muscle test, the hemisphere is switched on. If I record a weak muscle test, the Left Hemisphere is switched off. I would do likewise to check the condition of the Right Hemisphere.

Checking the hemispheres of the brain allows me to determine how the player would function while engaged in the activity for which we are muscle testing. For example, if I muscle tested you for scoring 20 points per game, and you had your Left Hemisphere switched on and your Right Hemisphere switched off, your Left Hemisphere would dominate your approach to the goal. You would exhibit the personality traits and attributes listed under the Left Hemisphere of the brain. You will try to use "old" information.

For instance, what did I do last week to score 20 points; what did I do the week before to score 20 points; Etc. It's as if you are walking through a mental revolving door. You keep creating the same experience (8 points per game). Without the participation of your Right Hemisphere you would be lacking information such as intuition, creativity and imagination. The end result - 8 points per game.

Thirdly, and most importantly, muscle testing allows me to validate, through post testing, that the stress relating to the subject matter has been cleared from the player's physical body. If I have you say "I consistently score 20 points per game," and you muscle test weak, and then have you say it again, and you muscle test strong, something obviously changed in your physical body and the way it reacted to the statement.

In HK, muscle testing allows me access a player's Subconscious Mind. If subconsciously stored information is to be changed, it must be done subconsciously. Muscle testing allows me to inferentially (indirectly) access information from a player's Subconscious Mind using his physical body. That's because the Mind and the physical body are integral and mirror each other. What affects the Mind affects the physical body, and vice versa.

When the physical body is in a weakened state, it is engaged in a phenomenon known as "sabotage." Muscle testing allows me to interpret the language used by the physical body to communicate this sabotage state, and that language is "stress."

Stress

Taber's Cyclopedic Medical Dictionary defines stress as, "...the result produced when a structure, system or organism is acted upon by forces that disrupt equilibrium or produce strain...the term denotes the physical and psychological forces that are experienced by individuals." Stress has an absolutely pervasive effect on the physical body, and the prolonged presence of stress in the body can manifest pathologically (disease).

When stress is present in the physical body, it creates a myriad of physiological changes. Some of the more salient physical reactions to stress are:

* Increase in the rate and force of heartbeat;
* A rise in systolic blood pressure;
* Sweating of the palms and hands;
* Dilation of the pupils;
* Decreased digestion;
* Blood distribution from less to more active organs;
* Increased blood glucose (hyperglycemia);
* Etc;

Can you imagine standing at the free throw line with 2 seconds left in the championship game with the score tied, and trying to make the shot with all this activity going on in your body? When stress is present in the physical body, it interrupts the electrical signals between the brain and muscles causing the body to weaken. It is when the body is in this weakened state that the sabotaging phenomenon occurs.

It is when the body is in this weakened state during a game that you will miss a shot that you have made a hundred times in practice. Or, make some mental error at a crucial point in the game. This sabotaging phenomenon is so subtle that you will be totally unaware that you are doing it because it is all happening subjectively or subconsciously. That is to say that it is happening below your level of conscious awareness.

The presence of stress in a player's physical body adversely affects him both physically and mentally. Physically, by weakening or switching off one or both sides of his physical body; and mentally, by weakening or switching off one or both hemispheres of his brain. When stress is present in a player's physical body, something is motivating his body to manifest stress. That something is a Synthesizing Event.

Synthesizing Events

A "synthesizing event" is created when the emotions from a traumatic experience actually synthesizes (comes together) with the information as it is being stored in the Subconscious Mind. This synthesized information remains stored and dormant in the Subconscious Mind until the Conscious Mind engages in some activity relative to the information. Once the Conscious Mind accesses this synthesized information, it will manifest in a player's physical body as stress.

One of the best analogies I have ever heard in describing, synthesizing events is to imagine yourself buying a brand new boat. The hull of this boat is clean and spotless. As you travel on water, barnacles will attach themselves to the hull. The more barnacles that attach to the hull, the slower the boat will travel, until the boat accumulates so many barnacles it stops all together.

Synthesizing events are like barnacles that have attached themselves to the hulls of our lives. If you accumulate enough barnacles they may manifest as a nervous breakdown, or some chronic illness. The barnacle analogy is likened to mental baggage that people carry around with them for years, and it adversely affects every aspect of their lives. When you accumulate too much mental baggage, the bottom falls out and you will have to take one of the many anti-depressants on the market just to make it through the day.

What's responsible for creating synthesizing events? Trauma! Webster's defines trauma as, "1. A bodily injury or shock; 2. An emotional shock, often having lasting psychic effects." As you can clearly see, trauma can be experienced both physically and mentally, and can range from mild to severe. The physical trauma from dislocating a shoulder during competition, for example, will heal with time.

However, the mental (emotional) trauma from the injury may stay in the player's physical body for years. How about this scenario? You are playing in a championship game with a 1-point lead and 2 seconds left on the clock, and a player on the other team throws a Hail Mary ball and it goes in and your team loses. The resulting emotional trauma from that loss stored in your Subconscious Mind as a synthesizing event and may adversely affect your play for years.

There are two types of synthesizing events. The "initial synthesizing event," and the "subsequent synthesizing event." The following analogy explains. Suppose you had a fear of heights. There was a first time you experienced that fear and it is referred to as the initial synthesizing event because it was the first time the synthesizing dynamics came into play relating to the subject matter.

That synthesized information is stored in your Subconscious Mind, and will remain dormant until you go near a high place again. Once this happens, the Conscious Mind sends instructions to the Subconscious Mind, "Send me all the information you have stored relating to being near a high place."

The stored information from the first experience comes up, and since an emotion has synthesized with the information, it comes up as well. Your first reaction is, "Let's get away from this ledge!" The second experience created a subsequent synthesizing event.

Once you have left harms' way and are in a safe place, the initial synthesizing event is once again stored in your Subconscious Mind, and the subsequent synthesizing event is stored for the first time. Now you have two subconsciously stored pieces of information (or experiences) to support your fear of heights, and so on.

Imagine an onion. Its center represents the kind of player you have the potential to become. Over the years you have accumulated layers of mental baggage (synthesizing events) that are responsible for the problems you are now experiencing with your athletic performance.

If you don't get rid of them now your onion will continue to grow and you will carry it with you from competition to competition. In order to access the center of your onion (your true potential), the layers of mental baggage must be peeled away, and that is exactly what HK and this program will help you do.

Please remember that it is not what you are doing, but where you are doing it. For instance, if I were to take a 12" wide plank and connect two buildings 5 feet off the ground and ask you to walk across it. No problem. If I moved that same plank up to the 30th floor and asked you to walk across it I would surely get a different response. It is not what you are doing, but where you are doing it.

It is my belief that 95% of all synthesizing events are stored in your Subconscious Mind during a period in your childhood development known as the Egocentric Stage.

The Egocentric Stage

There is a period in your childhood known as the egocentric stage, and it occurs between conception and 7 to 8 years of age. It was during this stage in your development when most of the synthesizing events were stored in your Subconscious Mind.

Webster's defines egocentricity as, "Regarding the self or the individual as the center of all things; Having little or no regard for interests or feelings other than one's own; Self-centered." The egocentric child is so self-centered that the first thought they have when something goes wrong in their lives is, "What did I do wrong?"

If you ask a three-year-old boy if he has a brother, he will answer yes. If you ask that same three-year-old boy if his brother has a brother, he will answer no. That's because the egocentric child cannot objectify his experience, he can only experience.

It's as if he cannot see himself. The reason for this phenomenon is that the egocentric child's Mind does not possess a critical factor. Remember that the critical factor allows your Mind to accept or reject incoming information passing through your Conscious Mind.

Without the capacity to criticize incoming information, the egocentric child's Subconscious Mind stores everything! At age 7 or 8 the child's critical factor starts kicking in. During the child's teen years, it is operating at full capacity because teenagers know everything and adults know nothing.

After the teen years, our criticalness starts reversing and by middle age, most of us experience a softening of our attitudes and come to realize that criticism was all a waste of good energy to begin with.

The absence of the critical factor also denies the egocentric child the capacity to rationalize. You cannot rationalize with someone who is incapable of objectifying his experiences. Some of the other anomalies associated with the egocentric child:

* Absolutize – You either love me or you hate me;
* Personalize - Takes everything personally;
* Idealize their role models – If dad says I'm stupid, it must be true;
* Self-blame – What did I do wrong;
* Shame – There must be something wrong with me;

Children have very limited resources when dealing with trauma. The only way they know how to deal with trauma is to block it out. They accomplish this by switching off one or both hemispheres of their brains depending on the severity of the trauma. This switching off will influence the decisions they make for the rest of their lives.

In the 1980's John Bradshaw brought to light much information relating to dysfunctional families. In a dysfunctional family, the members are simply not getting their needs met. But, what kind of a family environment would produce a functional child or adult? The following quote is from a book titled Trauma and Recovery by Dr. Judith Herman:

"The developing child's positive sense of self depends upon a caretaker's benign use of power. When a parent, who is so much more powerful than a child, nevertheless shows some regard for that child's individuality and dignity, that child feels valued and respected; he develops self-esteem. He also develops autonomy, that is, a sense of his own separateness within a relationship. He learns to control and regulate his own bodily functions and to form and express his own point of view."

Wouldn't it have been nice to have been raised in this environment? The truth is that 99% of all families are dysfunctional. This dysfunction leaves most children who experience it filled with shame and doubt. Dr. Herman continues:

"Shame is a response to helplessness, the violation of bodily integrity, and the indignity suffered in the eyes of another person. Doubt reflects the inability to maintain one's own separate point of view while remaining in connection with others. In the aftermath of traumatic events, survivors doubt both others and themselves."

If you show a child respect that child will learn to respect himself and others. Disrespect traumatizes him and creates a synthesizing event. As that child is creating a self-image, the synthesizing event will no doubt play a significant role in determining how that child will perceive himself. The trauma that created this switching off anomaly for the child doesn't make him functional, it makes him <u>more</u> functional in that he is having to compensate.

Here is an extraordinary example of how things we learn about ourselves during the egocentric stage of our development stay with us the rest of our lives. One day a teacher asked her students to list the names of the other students in the room on two sheets of paper, leaving a space between each name. Then she told them to think of the nicest thing they could say about each of their classmates and write it down. It took the remainder of the class period to finish their assignment, and as the students left the room, each one handed in the papers.

That Saturday, the teacher wrote down the name of each student on a separate sheet of paper, and listed what everyone else had said about that individual. On Monday she gave each student his or her list. Before long, the entire class was smiling. 'Really?' she heard whispered. "I never knew that I meant anything to anyone!" and, "I didn't know others liked me so much," were most of the comments.

No one ever mentioned those papers in class again. She never knew if the students discussed them after class or with their parents, but it didn't matter. The exercise had accomplished its purpose. The students were happy with themselves and one another. That group of students moved on.

Several years later, one of the students was killed in Viet Nam and his teacher attended the funeral of that special student. She had never seen a serviceman in a military coffin before. He looked so handsome, so mature. The church was packed with his friends. One by one those who loved him took a last walk by the coffin. The teacher was the last one to bless the coffin.

As she stood there, one of the soldiers who acted as pallbearer came up to her. "Were you Mark's math teacher?" he asked. She nodded, "Yes." Then he said, "Mark talked about you a lot." After the funeral, most of Mark's former classmates went together to a luncheon. Mark's mother and father were there, obviously waiting to speak with his teacher. "We want to show you something," his father said, taking a wallet out of his pocket. "They found this on Mark when he was killed. We thought you might recognize it."

Opening the billfold, he carefully removed two worn pieces of notebook paper that had obviously been taped, folded and refolded many times. The teacher knew without looking that the papers were the ones on which she had listed all the good things each of Mark's classmates had said about him. 'Thank you so much for doing that," Mark's mother said, "'As you can see, Mark treasured it."

All of Mark's former classmates started to gather around. Charlie smiled rather sheepishly and said, "I still have my list. It's in the top drawer of my desk at home." Chuck's wife said, "Chuck asked me to put his in our wedding album." "I have mine too," Marilyn said, "It's in my diary." Then Vicki, another classmate, reached into her pocketbook, took out her wallet and showed her worn and frazzled list to the group. "I carry this with me at all times," Vicki said and without batting an eyelash, she continued, "I think we all saved our lists."

If you tell a 6 year old he isn't good enough, he has no way of stopping that information. It goes right into subconscious storage and will be used at some point in his future to create his self-image. If you treat that same 6 years with respect and tell him he is loved and cherished he will, likewise, store the information subconsciously and it will have a profound positive impact on his self-image, and he will carry it with him for the rest of his life.

Many children start their basket careers playing in youth league during the egocentric stage of their development. If you are a coach, please be ever mindful of what to tell these children whenever you interact with them. Because they respect you, the will believe everything you tell them.

Sometimes the trauma is so severe that it causes both hemispheres of the brain to weaken or switch off. This creates a condition known as Dissociation.

Dissociation

As we had mentioned earlier, children do not have a lot of options when dealing with trauma. Children deal with it by blocking it out. They accomplish this by switching off one or both hemispheres of their brains depending upon the severity of the trauma. When both hemispheres of the brain switch off it creates a condition known as "dissociation."

Dissociation occurs when specific mental functions become separated (or dissociated) from the mainstream of consciousness and, as a consequence, are lost to the individual's awareness and voluntary control. When a player, for instance, dissociates at the free throw line, he cannot feel (Right Hemisphere switched off), nor is there structure to his shot making or mental processes (Left Hemisphere switched off).

It's as if you are totally disconnected from your body. There is a way to help athletes keep both hemispheres of their brains switched on during competition and it involves achieving Critical Factor Bypass. This is accomplished with the use of the HK Performance Trigger.

The HK Performance Trigger

We now know that when an athlete experiences a traumatic encounter, the emotions from that trauma will synthesize with the information stored in his Subconscious Mind and adversely affect his future performances. In order to clear the synthesizing event, a desynthesis must occur. In order to reverse this process, I employ the HK Performance Trigger.

The HK Performance Trigger is used to release the trauma and all associated emotions connected to that trauma from the player's Subconscious Mind manifesting as stress in his physical body. In other words, the intention of the HK Performance Trigger is to sever the emotional trauma from the information stored in the player's Subconscious Mind creating the stress in his physical body. It works because "energy follows intention."

The HK Performance Trigger is used to create Critical Factor Bypass so that you may change the subconsciously stored information contributing to your performance problems. Every time you use the HK Performance Trigger you are changing information on a subconscious level. Or, to put it another way, you are peeling the onion. Your objective is to get to the center of the onion which is where you will find your true potential to play your best during competition.

The more you do something the better you get at it. So, the more you use the HK Performance Trigger, the stronger and more effective it becomes. The HK Performance Trigger was designed to help you peel away the mental blockages preventing you from playing your best during competition. Now, let's show you how to use HK to clear those blockages.

But first, let me explain why players struggle with performance during competition.

Why Players Struggle

Earlier I had mentioned that when there is stress present in your body, it will cause one or both hemispheres of your brain to weaken or switch off. This switching off phenomenon will cause you to become left brain or right brain dominant. This brain dominance will adversely affect your play both physically and mentally. It affects your shot making (physically), as well as your thought processes (mentally). Here's why.

When stress is present in your physical body, it causes it to weaken. The presence of stress in your physical body will also cause one or both hemispheres of your brain to weaken or switch off. It's as if your body's electrical system blows a fuse. This causes an interruption of the electrical impulse from your brain to the muscles responsible for executing physical movement.

The Right Hemisphere of your brain controls the left side of your physical body, while the Left Hemisphere of your brain controls the right side. When you execute a shot with both hemispheres switched on, it will more than likely go in. However, when you execute that same shot with one or both hemispheres switched off, you will more than likely miss it.

When your Right Hemisphere weakens or switches off during your shot making, it weakens the left side of your physical body. When you take a shot during a game with a weak left side, it dramatically alters and changes the mechanical dynamics of your shot and will cause you to miss an easy shot that you have made hundreds of time in practice. There is no way you can achieve any consistency with your shot making with your body in this weakened state.

This weakened or switched off state is so subtle it cannot be seen with the naked eye, and that is where muscle testing comes in. Remember that muscle testing allows me to determine whether stress is present in the body relating to a statement, thought or action. This switching off anomaly not only affects you physically, but mentally as well.

Remember that the left hemisphere of your brain provides you with logic, analysis and structure, while your right hemisphere provides you with creativity, intuition and the capacity to feel. One of the traits of the left hemisphere is that it is cautious. So, left brained dominant player will have a tendency to play too conservative or safe and pass the ball rather than take a shot.

One of the traits of the right hemisphere of the brain is that it has no structure or boundaries. Conversely, right brain dominant players will have a tendency to take risky low percentage shots. Ideally you want both hemispheres of your brain switched on during competition. The physical advantage is that your shot making will become more consistent because both sides of your physical body will remain strong during the execution of your shots.

The mental advantage to having both hemispheres of your brain switched on is that you will have access to logic, analysis and structure (left hemisphere), and creativity, intuition and feeling (right hemisphere). With access to information provided by both hemispheres, you will effectively deal with whatever situations you encounter during your game. You will also enter a mental and physical domain known as the "Zone."

The best way to enter the zone and remain there is to remain calm and relaxed. When you can remain calm and relaxed during competition your brain functions at maximum capacity, and you will have access to information provided by both hemispheres of your brain.

The intention of this program is to help you keep both hemispheres of your brain switched on during competition so that they both participate in allowing you to play your best. With both hemispheres of your brain contributing to your performance, you will not play too conservatively, nor will you play too aggressively. You will achieve a balance that will allow you make the necessary decisions on the court that support you in playing your best and helping your team win the game.

If you can remain calm and relaxed during your games, especially during pressure situations, you will have access to all the information necessary to help you implement whatever strategy your team has decided upon in order to win the game. It also allows you to keep both sides of your physical body strong so that you may experience the continuity in your play necessary to help your team win. The one thing that separates the good players from the great players is the five-inch space between their ears.

What you are about to learn in the following pages will help you remain calm, relaxed and focused during your games and help provide you with mental clarity so that the decisions you make on the court support you in doing your best to help your team win your game. You will be shown step by step:

1. How to program in the HK Performance Trigger;
2. How to use this trigger before, during and after your games;
3. How to use the *Mind Mastery For Basketball* program;
4. How to use the trigger during practice;
5. How to do the HK Journaling exercise after each game so that you don't carry mental baggage with you into your next game.

Let's first show you how to program in the HK Performance Trigger.

Programming In The HK Performance Trigger

There are three steps to programming in the HK Performance Trigger:

Step #1: Read the following statement aloud:

"I, (state your name), now accept and integrate into my mind and body the HK Trigger which is stating, thinking or hearing the word 'relax' and touching the thumb and index fingers of both hands, to immediately and permanently neutralize all initial and synthesizing events manifesting as stress in every cell, organ and tissue of my physical body, and to instantly and permanently 'switch on' the left and right hemispheres of my brain as well as my corpus callosum so that all three components function as one allowing me to always remain calm, relaxed and focused during all my basketball games, and to activate that part of my mind that supports me in helping my team win every game in which I compete, and to be open to receive more wealth, health, happiness, peace, joy, prosperity, safety and security in my life, and all other attributes I may require to help me experience the lifestyle of my choosing, to help me successfully accomplish all my goals, and to improve the quality of my life relating to every statement, thought and action I experience, layers one through infinity, and I will never interfere with the successful and physical manifestation of all my goals. This or something better."

Step #2: Say the word "relax" and touch the thumb and index fingers of both hands, then release and open your fingers.

<u>Step #3:</u> Read the statement in Step #1 again. Remember to read it aloud so that you involve as many of your senses as possible. The HK Performance Trigger, which is stating or thinking the word "relax" and touching the thumb and index fingers of both hands, is now programmed into your Subconscious Mind.

The HK Performance Trigger is intended to help you stay calm, relaxed and focused during your basketball games. When you can remain relaxed when you execute your shots and movements on the court, both hemispheres of your brain will remain switched on.

This helps keep both sides of your body strong allowing the proper execution of your movements whether they are offensive or defensive. It will also provide you with the mental clarity to help you create a strategy that will support you in playing your best. This ultimately results in more consistent play and dramatically enhances your team's chances of winning the game.

If the presence of stress in your physical body indicates that you are in a sabotage mode, then the intention of the HK Performance Trigger is to get you in a calm and relaxed state of mind during competition. When you can remain relaxed during your games you are experiencing peak performance because during this calm and relaxed state your brain functions at maximum capacity.

During this peak mental state, both your

Conscious and Subconscious Mind are on the same page. When your Conscious Mind decides to do XYZ, your Subconscious Mind will support you in doing it, and you will do it well.

The HK Trigger is designed to help you:

- Instantly, automatically and permanently release all trauma from your Conscious and Subconscious Mind manifesting as stress in your body;
- Instantly, automatically and permanently "switch on" and strengthen both hemispheres of your brain relating to every statement, thought or action you experience relating to your goal(s);
- Stay calm, focused and relaxed during competition;
- Clear all mental blockages preventing you from playing your best, and successfully accomplishing your personal and basketball related goals.

The reason the HK Performance Trigger is so effective is because "energy follows intention." Remember that the more you use the trigger, the stronger it becomes. There is an excellent process we use in HK to extract information from your Subconscious Mind. It is called HK Journaling.

HK Journaling

Remember that one of the limitations of the Conscious Mind is that it can only focus on one thing at a time. If you are having problems with your performances, there is usually more than one thing responsible for those problems. HK Journaling allows you to bring up those problems, or the negative experiences you had during your game, one at a time in order of their priority.

HK Journaling entails the use of open-ended statements to access subconsciously stored information manifesting as problems during your basketball games. Grab a pencil and a blank piece of paper and draw a line down the center of the page. At the top of the left side of the page write the word Negative. At the top of the right side of the page write the word Positive.

Using open-ended statements list the negative things that occurred for you during your game on the left side of the page. For instance, let's assume that you have just finished a basketball game and your team lost. Here is how you would document this information.

1. One of the negative things that occurred during my performance was: Our team lost the game;
2. The second negative thing that occurred during my performance was: I went 1 for 4 at the free throw line;
3. The third negative thing that occurred during my performance was: Etc.

After you have finished documenting all the negative things that occurred for you during your game, go to the top of the right side of the page and document all the positive things that occurred for you.

1.   One of the positive things that occurred during my performance was: I scored 22 points;
2.   The second positive thing that occurred during my performance was: I had 10 assists;
3.   The third positive thing that occurred during my performance was: Etc.

It is important to also focus on the positive things that occurred during your game because if you only focus on the negative that is all you will see. It reminds of an old saying I once heard, "You are never as good as you think you are, but you are never as bad either." Looking at both negative and positive elements of your game just gives you a more balanced perspective on what's really going on for you.

As you can clearly see, the HK Journaling exercise allows you to document a tremendous amount of information regarding your performance, and the problems that came up for you. If you went 1 for 4 at the free throw line, something motivated your body to miss those three shots. And, that something was mental, and that is what we want to clear using this process.

Now, let's discuss how the HK Performance Trigger is used to clear the information that surfaced for you during your post performance evaluations.

How To Use The HK Performance Trigger

With the onion analogy I explained that the center of the onion represents the type of player you have the potential to become. The layers of mental baggage in the form of synthesizing events that you have accumulated over the years, is responsible for preventing you from becoming that player. What's creating problems with your basketball game right now is the fact that you carry this mental baggage with you from game to game. It's as if you are walking through a mental revolving door.

I suggest that you do the HK Journaling exercise the evening after each and every game in which you compete. What follows is a four step process that will allow you to peel away the layers of mental blockages responsible for creating the problems you are now experiencing with your basketball game:

Step #1: If you haven't already, go back to the chapter on Programming In The HK Performance Trigger. Program in the trigger by following Steps 1 through 3;

Step #2: Read your HK Journaling list starting with the negative things that came up for you during your basketball game and read them one at a time;

Step #3: After reading the first item on the negative side of your list, hit your trigger. Say or mentally state the word "relax" and touch the thumb and index fingers of both your hands, and open them. Move to the second negative thing and do the same thing until you have gone through the entire negative list;

Step #4:   Now, move to the positive list and repeat Step #3 until you have gone through the entire positive list;

This is extremely effective because your Subconscious Mind stored every aspect of your performance earlier that day. Doing the HK Journaling exercise allows you to access that information from your Subconscious Mind and any mental blockages attached to it. Using the HK Performance Trigger creates a space whereby you can clear and release those synthesizing events manifesting as mental blockages so that you don't carry them with you into your next game.

Here's why this is so effective. Suppose one of the negative things that came during your post game HK Journaling was that you went 1 of 4 at the free throw line. When you read that statement, your Conscious Mind will send instructions to your Subconscious Mind, "Send up all the information you have in storage relating to going 1 for 4 at the free throw line."

When that information comes up from your Subconscious Mind, it will bring all the mental baggage (synthesizing events) associated with it as well. When you hit your HK Performance Trigger, it allows you to subconsciously clear away yet another layer of this mental onion that has grown around your basketball game.

My suggestion is to punch holes in the completed journaling forms and keep them in a three ring binder. Once a month or so, review them and see if you can find any patterns that may be developing in your game that may need addressing. In fact, the question you should be asking yourself after each game is, "What could I have done to improve my play during this game?"

If you don't think this process is effective, Byron Nelson, a former PGA Tour player, won 18 tournaments (11 in a row!) in one year back in the 1940's doing the exact same thing. If it worked for him, it will certainly work for you.

The HK Performance Trigger can also be used during your basketball games as a Pre-Shot Routine.

The Pre-Shot Routine

You will be integrating this pre-shot routine into your basketball games for one reason and one reason only, to help you become as calm and relaxed as possible during the execution of your shots on basket. When you are relaxed during the execution of your shots, it allows you to keep both hemispheres of your brain switched on. This keeps both sides of your physical body strong allowing you to mechanically execute your shots with continuity and consistency.

Here's how you do the pre-shot routine before a shot on basket:

1.   Before you execute your shot, mentally state your goal for the shot (i.e., my goal is to put this shot in the basket);
2.   Mentally state the word "relax" and proceed to execute your shot;

There are many reasons why this pre-shot routine is so effective. The most important reason is that it allows you to remain focused on your whole purpose for being out there, and that is to play your best and help your team win the game. It also allows you to set a goal for each shot, and the continued use of the HK Performance Trigger will help you stay relaxed.

Another excellent advantage in using this pre-shot routine is a phenomenon known as "compounding." Compounding occurs when the same suggestion is layered upon itself many times. The incessant use of the word relax will eventually condition your body to relax. Your play will become much more consistent, and you may even begin to enjoy the experience.

The HK Performance Trigger can be used for both offensive as well as defensive goals during your game. Throughout the game continually remind yourself to relax. The HK Performance Trigger can also be used when you are sitting on the bench.

Using The HK Trigger on The Bench

The HK Performance Trigger can also be used when another player replaces you during a game. You can perform a quick mini evaluation of the minutes you have just played. The intention of this procedure is to prevent you from carrying mental baggage from one playing stint to the next.

For example, let's say that you have just completed a five-minute stint of playing time and you missed two jump shots and a free throw. As you are sitting on the bench, ask yourself, "Why did I miss those three shots?" Then mentally state the word relax. This allows you to subconsciously access and clear the mental blockage that was responsible for causing you to miss your shots on basket.

Here's why this works. When you asked the question about your missed shots, your Conscious Mind sent instructions to your Subconscious Mind, "Send me all the information you have in storage relating to the three shots I just missed?"

When that information comes up from your Subconscious Mind, it will bring all the mental baggage (synthesizing events) associated with it as well. When you hit your HK Performance Trigger, it allows you to clear away yet another layer of this mental onion that has grown around your basketball game.

Remember that it has taken you years to create and accumulate these layers around the core of this onion, and that you have been carrying around this mental baggage for a long time. Continued use of the HK Performance Trigger will help to accelerate the removal of these layers of mental blockages responsible for your marginal play during your basketball games.

Your physical body never does anything arbitrarily. If you miss a shot that causes you to lose an important game, for instance, something motivated your body to do that. During any breaks in the action, do a quick mini evaluation of your playing minutes to access any anomalies that may have surfaced for you during your performance and use your HK Performance Trigger to clear them.

This prevents you from carrying the mental baggage responsible for your missing that important shot into your next game situation.

Mind Mastery For Basketball

I created program for basketball players called *Mind Mastery For Basketball.* It includes the DVD *Change Your Thinking, Change Your Life,* and a powerful 30 minute CD titled *Winning At Basketball.* The DVD explains how I use muscle testing when working with individuals to help them clear blockages preventing them from successfully accomplishing their goals.

The CD *Winning At Basketball* is designed and intended to work on a subconscious level. The HK Trigger word (relax) is programmed in at the beginning of the CD. The CD contains over 100 statements relating specifically to basketball and winning. Each statement is followed by the trigger word "relax."

For instance, one of the statements on the CD is, "Release all fear from your mind and body preventing you from winning at basketball." This statement, and all statements on the CD, are followed with the trigger word relax. Any subconsciously stored fear relating to the statement will surface, and the trigger word relax is simply a medium that will allow you to subconsciously release it.

The reason it works is because "Energy Follows Intention!" The intention of the trigger is to clear all stress from your body relating to every statement contained on the CD. Repeated listening to the CD will help you peel away layers of mental blockages from this subconscious onion you have created over the years impeding your success as a basketball player. Here is what you do. Find a quiet location to sit or recline.

Close your eyes and do your best to consciously listen to each statement. Pay close attention to any physiological changes or sensations you may experience in your body after hearing the trigger word relax. You may find yourself taking a deep breath or yawning. This simply means that a very subtle energy shift is occurring for you on a subconscious level relating to one of the statements you just heard.

It is recommended that you listen to the CD before and after each game. The CD is designed to work on a subconscious level because that is where your performance problems are. Listening to the CD before your games helps you to mentally prepare by clearing out the cobwebs. Listening to the CD after your games helps to peel away layers of mental blockages that may have surfaced for you during your performance. This may manifest in your game as low point production, or making a mental error at a crucial point in the game.

Think of your age. That's how old your belief system is. If for instance, you can only average 8 points a game, it is simply your belief system acting out through your physical body. And, it will continue to perpetuate your low point production until something changes. Listening to the CD daily allows you to peel away the layers of this onion manifesting for you as 8 points a game.

Remember that when stress is present in your body it will also cause one or both hemispheres of your brain to weaken or switch off. It is when the brain is in this weakened state that the sabotaging anomaly will manifest for you. Listening to the CD coupled with the HK Journaling exercise will provide you with an excellent regimen to help you accelerate the peeling away of the layers of negative information preventing you from reaching your true potential to become a premier player at your position.

I cannot stress the important of listening to the CD every day you touch a basketball. Even after practice. Sometimes it is difficult for you to take 30 minutes out of your day to sit down and listen to the CD. If this is the case, I suggest that you buy a small portable CD player and place it at the head of you bed. Turn it on before you drift off to sleep with the volume low.

Although the best results will be achieved from listening to the CD while in your waking conscious state, you will still derive substantial benefits from listening to it as you drift off to sleep. Also, it wouldn't hurt to have the whole team listen to the CD before the start of the game.

It simply helps to puts every team member on the same page mentally. Listening to the CD allows you to do everything in your power to become mentally prepared for your upcoming game.

Setting Goals

After Tiger Woods won his first Masters he took a week off and came back and won the next tournament. During his post tournament interview, he was asked why he thought he won the tournament. He looked at the interviewer surprisingly and replied, *"Because it was my goal to win it."*

How does your physical body know what your mind expects from it if you do not set a goal? I hate to use cliques, but this one is so appropriate. When you don't set goals, it is like a ship without a rudder. It just spins in circles. Even if your physical body sabotages your efforts, give it the benefit of the doubt and ALWAYS SET GOALS!

Always set a goal to win before each game. Here's how you would document your goals before a game. Grab a piece of paper and write your goal to get as many senses involved as possible:

1. I, (write your name), will do my best to help my team win our upcoming game against (write the name of your opponent) by remaining calm, relaxed, focused and balanced, and by playing my best at all times;
2. I, will do my best, during this game, to score 20 or more points, grab 10 or more rebounds, and 10 or more assists; Etc.
3. I will do everything in my power to successfully accomplish all my goals. This or something better.

Here's how you would use the HK Trigger for

your game goals:

Step 1: Read your first goal aloud and hit your HK Trigger by stating or thinking the word "relax" and touching the thumb and index fingers of both your hands and opening them.

Step 2: Read your first goal again.

Step 3: Read the second goal and repeat steps 1 and 2 until you have finished reading the entire list.

Repeating this process before every game allows your mind an opportunity to communicate your intentions to your physical body that your goal is to help your team win. Now, if you do not achieve the point production you documented in your goal, it simply means that your mental onion needs additional peeling. You still have mental blockages that need to be cleared. Please do your best to remain objective during this process.

Doing the HK Journaling exercise, setting goals and listening to the CD will help you on the road to becoming the kind of player you would like to become by peeling away the layers of mental blockages stopping you from realizing your goals.

Before you run out to the court to take you warm-ups, every player on your team should set a goal to win the game. The reason this is so powerful is that it allows every player to verbalize the team goal to win the game, but it also puts every team player on the same page. And, that is, or should be, to win the game. ALWAYS SET A GOAL TO WIN THE GAME!

Using Your Imagination During Practice

Imagination is defined as, "The action or faculty of forming mental images or concepts of what is not actually present to the senses." When you imagine yourself doing something, you are going to subconsciously access the same information as if you were actually physically doing it. Using your imagination during practice has a twofold benefit.

First, since your imagination is located in the right hemisphere of your brain, every time you use it you are exercising that part of your brain. If you can keep the right hemisphere of your brain switched on during your practice sessions, you will keep it switched on during your games.

Secondly, your Subconscious Mind cannot distinguish between something real or imagined. Using imagination in conjunction with the HK Performance Trigger allows you to clear any mental baggage you may have stored relating to a particular game situation.

Think of the most stressful situation you normally encounter during a game, and mentally imagine yourself in that situation during practice. For instance, imagine that you are playing in the final of the NBA Championships or the final of the NCAA Basketball Championships, and the score is tied with 2 seconds left in the game.

See if you can make the shot. If you miss it, chances are you would miss it during a real game situation. Simply ask yourself, "Why did I miss that shot to win the game and the championship?"

Then hit your HK Performance Trigger by mentally stating or thinking the word "relax". Keep mentally creating that situation until you make the shot. Then move on to other stressful situations you encounter during your games and repeat the same procedure. If you can find another player who is close to your level, mentally create game situations and play the point.

Imagination is so effective that during the final round of the 1994 United States Women's Open Golf Championships, Lauri Merten was on the putting green imagining herself putting to win the tournament. Four hours later she was hoisting the trophy as the 1994 United States Women's Golf Open champion. Imagination is a very powerful and effective tool, and it works. I entreat you to religiously integrate it into your practice regime.

Conclusion

I don't specifically know what you are going to have to do to become the kind of basketball player you want to become, but on some level of your awareness you do. Using this program faithfully will help you peel away those mental blockages preventing you from accessing that information so that you can realize your potential to become a premier player at your position.

To gain maximum benefit from this program it is important to use the entire program, which entails:

• Programming in the HK Performance Trigger;
• Setting goals and using your HK Performance Trigger to clear blockages;
• Faithfully using the HK Journaling exercise after each game documenting negative and positive information relating to your performances;
• Listening to the CD Winning At Basketball before and after each game.

In closing, please remember that we dealing with a tremendous amount of information in your Subconscious Mind relating to your basketball career that has been stored over a period of many years. Please do your best to remain objective while using this program.

I hope this book has given you a perspective that will allow you to more fully understand how your Mind and physical body influence your performance as a basketball player. And, that I have provided you with a discipline that can accelerate positive changes for you that will help you achieve peak performance, not only during your basketball games, but ultimately improve the quality of your personal life as well.

It is said that, "Adversity introduces a man to himself." I trust that when you encounter adversity on the court or in your personal life, that you will not only know where it came from, but remain objective enough to conquer it effectively using HK.

A wise man once wrote *"We can't be Batman to all the Robins in the world."* You cannot control what others think of you, but you can control what you think about you. And, believe you me, that will be a full time job. Please remember that basketball, like life, is relative, and that among the blind, the one eyed man is King. "Relax."

***

HK Mind Mastery programs:

Mind Mastery For Golf
Mind Mastery For Soccer
Mind Mastery For Tennis
Mind Mastery For Hitting
Mind Mastery For Pitching
Mind Mastery For Coaching
Mind Mastery For Basketball
Mind Mastery For Winning
Mind Mastery For Money
Mind Mastery For Selling
Mind Mastery For Learning
Mind Mastery For Weight Loss
Mind Mastery For Peace of Mind
Change Your Thinking Change Your Life

Other books by Ernest Solivan:

Mastering The Mental Side of Soccer
Mastering The Mental Side of Tennis
Mastering The Mental Side of Hitting
Mastering The Mental Side of Football
Mastering The Mental Side of Pitching
Mastering The Mental Side of Coaching
Mastering The Mental Side of Winning
Mastering The Mental Side of Basketball
Mastering The Mental Side of Putting
Mastering The Mental Side of Tournament Golf
Pro Se Cites & Authorities

For more information about Hemispheric
Kinesiology contact:
Performance Consultants International
Website: www.hk-relax.com

Relax!

www.ingramcontent.com/pod-product-compliance
Lightning Source LLC
Chambersburg PA
CBHW021341090426
42742CB00008B/690